# START·A·CRAFT

# Basketmaking

Get started in a new craft with easy-to-follow

projects for beginners

POLLY POLLOCK

THE
APPLE
PRESS

A QUINTET BOOK

Published by The Apple Press
6 Blundell Street
London N7 9BH

ISBN 1-85076-506-5

This book was designed and produced by
Quintet Publishing Limited
6 Blundell Street
London N7 9BH

Creative Director: Richard Dewing
Designer: Ian Hunt
Project Editor: Stefanie Foster
Copy Editor: Michelle Clark
Illustrator: Jeremy Siddall
Photographer: Ian Howes

Typeset in Great Britain by
Central Southern Typesetters, Eastbourne
Manufactured in Hong Kong by
Regent Publishing Services Limited
Printed in China
Leefung-Asco Printers Limited

**DEDICATION**

Granwin, Granpa and MM

# Contents

# Introduction

Basketry is an ancient craft, probably predating even pottery and textiles, which has a history going back many thousands of years.

Very early baskets were likely to have been crude throwaway containers — like early carrier bags, perhaps — made on the spot as the need arose, to hold and transport gathered food, for example. Such baskets are still made today. In parts of Southeast Asia, for example, you may still be given a roughly woven palm-leaf basket to carry your shopping home in rather than a plastic bag. This type of basket is made from whatever is easily available and is suited to weaving quickly into the required form.

Basketry has evolved over the centuries as a response to this need to protect and contain things, from eggs to rubbish. The specific forms reflect the wide-ranging yet particular uses that it has served — traps to catch fish and lobsters, baskets and mats used when preparing or serving food, baskets to transport racing pigeons, hats to protect their wearers from the sun and rain, even simple houses, and last, but not least, baskets for carrying all sorts of things in. If you visit a museum with an ethnographic section, you are likely to see some of the surprising and varied functions that basketry fulfils.

As well as being an ancient craft, basketry is an almost universal one, many of its forms and techniques having evolved independently in different parts of the world. The different techniques used to make baskets largely reflects the materials available to the makers. Although there are many variations within basketry techniques, they can be grouped into five main categories:

◊ stake and strand
◊ plaiting/checkweave
◊ coiling
◊ twining
◊ knotting and netting

This book introduces the first three.

### STAKE AND STRAND

This technique is used with rigid materials such as willow, bamboo and cane. Cane is used for four projects in this book.

Cane is the stem of the climbing palm generally known as rattan, imported mainly from Southeast Asia. By the time it reaches the user, it has gone through several processes to produce long strands tied in 1lb/½kg hanks. One of these involves milling it to produce the different thicknesses, categorized according to the diameter of the strand and measured in millimetres. The size categories range from very, very fine (No. 000, which is 1mm in diameter) to middle range (No. 5, which is 2.5mm, and No. 6, which is 2.65mm), right up to handle cane (which is 8mm or 10mm in diameter). The size used will depend, first, on the planned size and function of the basket and, second, the position and function of the cane in the basket, so, for example, base sticks are thicker than side stakes.

Processed cane has a neutral, creamy colour, which can be rather dull and lifeless, although there are weaves that produce interesting textures. However, as cane takes some dyes very easily, all sorts of possibilities for colour and pattern are there to be explored.

### PLAITING

Plaiting uses materials that are naturally (or can be made into) long, flat, ribbon-like strips, such as palm leaves or birch bark.

Basketmakers have always used whatever materials they could find easily and which could be used for weaving. In modern, urban environments, one such material available to the ecologically minded basketmaker is discarded cardboard boxes. Painted and cut up into long strips, they are an ideal material for plaited baskets — and they are free!

### COILING

While there are some similarities between the stake and strand and plaiting techniques, the technique of coiling is unique. Even though the techniques are different, the materials used are often the same or similar. For instance, lengths of split palm leaves can be used for stitching around a core bundle of straw or grasses. Some materials are used for both stitching and core material, such as raffia, which comes from the leaves of the raffia palm.

## HOW TO USE THIS BOOK

This book is divided into three sections, distinguished from each other by the materials and techniques used.

In each section, the first project is the most straightforward and introduces basic techniques. Subsequent projects introduce additional techniques as well as consolidating the skills already learned. For example, in order to weave the Cylindrical Basket on page 19, it is helpful to have made several bases and to have practised the weaves, which are introduced in the Placemat and Tablemat projects that precede it. So, if you are a beginner, you can expect better results if you build on your skills progressively rather than starting straight away, say, with the Shopping Basket on page 23.

Before starting any of the projects, read the introduction to that section as this gives important information about techniques you will need to know when working on each basket. When a technique is introduced in the step-by-step instructions, it will appear in italics, e.g. now *make the slath*. This indicates that you should refer to that technique at the beginning of the chapter.

It is also very useful to read the instructions for the project all the way through before starting so you have an overall picture in your mind of what you are doing and how this relates to the other steps and the appearance of the finished basket.

Regarding tools and equipment, no great investment is required as you do not need many items and the ones you do need are "low-tech". Indeed, you may well have all the necessary things already; for example, scissors, string, clothes-pegs. For those items you do not have immediate access to, it is usually possible to improvise until you are able to buy or borrow the tools mentioned. For example, you could use a skewer instead of a bodkin.

## A NOTE FOR LEFTHANDED BASKETMAKERS

All the projects are described with a righthanded person in mind, that is, working from left to right. It is much easier for a lefthanded person to work right to left and there is no reason why this can't be done, but for reasons of space it wasn't possible to include reverse instructions in this book.

## FINAL NOTE

I hope that you enjoy making these projects and, equally important, that you enjoy using them, too.

# USING CANE

## INTRODUCTION

The sizes of cane used for the four projects in this section are:

◊ handle cane (8 or 10mm)
◊ No. 14
◊ No. 11
◊ No. 8
◊ No. 5

If you cannot find the exact cane sizes specified for a particular project, one size up or down from that given will almost certainly work just as well. For example, the difference between No. 5 (2.5mm) and No. 6 (2.65mm) cane is negligible – 0.15mm!

## THE TECHNIQUES YOU NEED TO KNOW TO MAKE THE PROJECTS

Several techniques are common to the projects that follow and these are explained below. In the projects, the techniques used are listed beneath the materials and references to them in the step-by-step instructions are printed in italics where they first occur. Until you are familiar with the various techniques, it is best to read through the relevant sections below before starting a project, as there are all sorts of tips and clear explanations to help you achieve the best results. These are not described in such detail in the projects.

## PREPARING CANE FOR USE

Cane should always be worked when it is wet because, in its dry state, it is quite brittle. However, too much soaking can badly discolour the cane, so, whenever possible, use hot water for soaking cane. If you have to use cold water, you will need to soak the cane for a bit longer.

As a rough guide, the thicker sizes of cane need to soak for a maximum of about 5 to 10 minutes in hot water. The thinner the cane, the less soaking time it will need. Try to get used to how long to soak the various sizes of cane by feel. It is ready to use when you can bend it through a 90° angle without it breaking. However, some cane will always crack a little no matter what you do to soften it.

To keep the cane damp while the project is in progress, use a shower or plant spray if possible in preference to soaking it again.

Remember *never* to leave cane to dry in an airless place, such as in a plastic bag, as it will become mouldy in a surprisingly short space of time.

### Cutting cane

Get into the habit of cutting cane on a slant. Apart from a few exceptions it is very useful to have a point at the end of a piece of cane as it is easier to insert it into previous weaving or thread through gaps as required.

## Dyeing cane

In its natural state, basketry cane is a creamy-white colour. Cane takes dye very well and it is interesting to experiment with the colour patterns different weaves produce. An added advantage is that you can make something to fit in with the colour scheme of a particular room.

It does not take long to dye cane, but it is very important that the safety precautions detailed in the dyeing instructions are followed exactly and that you work in a well-ventilated room.

You can either use the dyed cane immediately or leave it in a dry, airy place to dry out. Note that you should never leave damp cane in a plastic bag as it will become mouldy.

### You will need
◊ Face mask
◊ Rubber gloves
◊ Old metal pan or bucket (not to be re-used for holding food as toxic traces can remain)
◊ Suitable dye (enough to dye about 1lb/½kg of cane)
◊ Mordant—some salt for hot-water dyes, but read the manufacturer's instructions
◊ Kettle and water
◊ Stick
◊ Newspaper

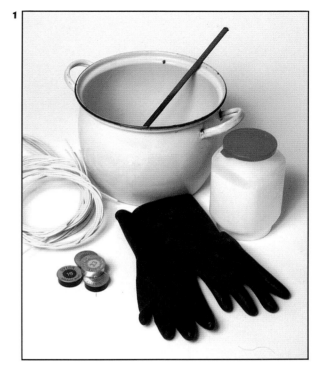

1 Wind 2 or 3 strands of cane round into a bundle and do the same with the rest of the cane. Don't make the bundles too tight or you will get a tie-dye effect. Soak the bundles in hot water for about 5 minutes.

2 Prepare the dye solution. Put on the face mask and rubber gloves, then, in the pan or bucket, mix together the dye, the mordant and water according to the manufacturer's instructions. Stir well with a stick.

3 Put the soaked bundles of cane into the dye. To ensure that the cane is dyed evenly, don't put too many bundles in at once, and keep it moving.

4 When the cane is a good strong colour, rinse it well under cold running water.

## WEAVING A ROUND BASE
### Making the slath

The number of sticks used will vary from project to project — the instructions that follow give an example of making slath for a round-based basket, using the "stake and strand" technique.

1 Cut 8 sticks to the length required for the diameter of the base plus 1½–2in/4–5cm.

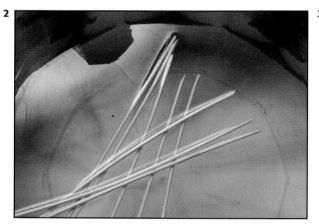

2 Soak the sticks in warm to hot water for 5 to 10 minutes to soften them.

3 Pierce through the centre of 1 stick using a bodkin and push it along the bodkin. Repeat this process with 3 more sticks so that you have 4 sticks on the bodkin.

4 Without removing the bodkin, thread 1 of the remaining sticks through the pierced sticks. Then, remove the bodkin and thread the remaining 3 sticks through the hole.

### Tying in the slath

1 Take a length of soaked cane, bend it at the centre and loop it around 1 arm of the slath (see above). This is the first stage of "tying in the slath" and looks neatest when the loop of weaving cane lies parallel to the pierced sticks.

2 Holding the slath in your left hand, hold the weaving cane so that you have a righthand and lefthand strand. These strands are called "weavers". Hold down the righthand weaver with your left thumb and, working clockwise, take the lefthand weaver across the top arm of the slath, down behind the second arm, then

up, finishing at the front. Give the slath a quarter turn anticlockwise.

3 Repeat step 2, keeping the weaving as tight and neat as possible. Work 3 rows in this way. Now the process of "tying in the slath" is complete. The weave used for tying in the slath and for the rest of the base is called "pairing".

**Continuing the base**

4 The arms of the slath are now opened up into pairs. Do this by firmly pulling the sticks apart after working the last stroke of row 3 and bringing the weaver up to the front between the pairs of stakes.

5 Continue pairing, opening out the sticks until you have 8 evenly spaced pairs. Work 2 rows.

6 Then, continuing with pairing, open out all the sticks to singles. To keep the weaving tight and neat, as you take the lefthand weaver down and behind, pull downwards on the weaver. Take care to maintain this tension as you bring the weaver back to the front.

## WEAVES

### PAIRING

1 If beginning pairing after a block of waling (for the sides of the Cylindrical Basket, for example) lay 2 weavers – **a** and **b** – into 2 consecutive spaces, between stakes **1** and **2**, and **2** and **3**.

2 Take strand a, which is the lefthand weaver, in front of stake **2**, over the top of strand **b**, behind stake **3**, to lie between stakes **3** and **4**. Then take strand **b** – which is now the lefthand weaver – in front of stake **3**, over the top of

strand **a**, behind stake **4**, to lie between stakes **4** and **5**. Continue like this, always taking the lefthand weaver in front of one stake and then behind one stake. So **a** will travel in front of **6** and behind **7**, and so on.

### Joining In Pairing

1 When one of the existing weavers begins to run out – when there is about 2in/5cm left – you will need to join in a new weaver (in pairing, the weaver you are joining must always be the lefthand one). Join in the new weaver – **c** – as shown. Note that the new weaver is inserted towards the left of the space between stakes **1** and **2**, and goes under both the existing weavers **a** and **b**.

2 Pick up the new weaver – **c** – and continue pairing. Work it over the old end in front of stake **2** and behind stake **3**.

## Completing pairing

On the last stroke of the final round of pairing, as you bring the lefthand weaver back to the front, thread it under the top strand of the row below to secure it. The other weaver is automatically trapped during this process.

## THREE-ROD WALE

$1$ Lay 3 weavers (**a**, **b** and **c** in the diagram) in 3 consecutive spaces.

$2$ Mark the stake to the left of the lefthand weaver with a short length of string.

$3$ Take the lefthand weaver — **a** — in front of 2 stakes — **1** and **2** — over the top of weavers **b** and **c**, behind 1 stake — **3** — and out to the front in the space between stakes **3** and **4**. Note that the weavers all travel in front of 2 stakes, behind 1 — **remember this rule.**

$4$ Then, take weaver **b**, now the lefthand weaver, in front of 2 stakes — **2** and **3** — over weavers **c** and **a**, behind 1 stake — **4** — and out to the front between stakes **4** and **5**.

$5$ Take weaver **c** in front of 2 stakes — **3** and **4** — behind stake **5** and out to the front between stakes **5** and **6**. Continue in this way, always working with the lefthand weaver.

## Working a Step-up in a Three-rod Wale

When working waling weaves in cane it is common practice to work a "step-up" at the end of every row. This prevents the weave spiralling.

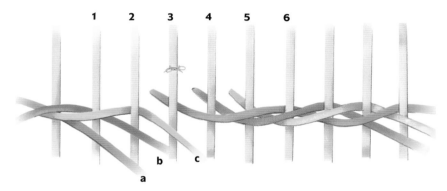

$1$ The diagram shows the position of the weavers just before the step-up is worked. Note that the righthand weaver — **c** — is in the space immediately to the left of the marked stake. For 3 strokes only, the weavers are worked in reverse order.

$2$ Take the righthand weaver — **c** — in front of stakes **3** and **4** and behind stake **5**.

3 Take the middle weaver – **b** – in front of stakes **2** and **3** and behind stake **4**.

4 Take the lefthand weaver – **a** – in front of stakes **1** and **2** and behind stake **3**. Weaver **a** now lies in the space immediately to the right of the marked stake. The step-up is now complete. The next row of waling can now be worked as explained above, starting with the lefthand weaver – **a**.

## Joining in a Three-rod Wale

1 Make sure that the weaver to be joined is the lefthand one – **A**.

2 Insert the new weaver – **a** – in the space between the old weaver – **A** – and stake **1**, so that it lies under weavers **b** and **c**.

3 Then, continue waling as before – in front of 2 stakes and behind 1 stake and so on. Never join at or near a step-up.

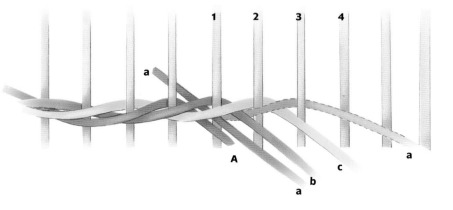

## Completing a Three-rod Wale

1 Work a step-up as explained above.

2 Thread each weaver under the top 2 strands of weaving as follows:
**a** under **b** and **c**
**b** under **a** and **c**
**c** under **a** and **b**

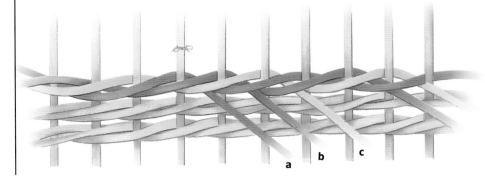

## FOUR-ROD WALE

As you might expect, this weave is very similar to a three-rod wale. The difference is that the weavers travel in front of 3 stakes before going behind 1, instead of in front of 2 stakes.

## Working a Step-up in a Four-rod Wale

This, too, is worked in almost the same way as for a three-rod step-up, except that there are 4 stages, each weaver travelling in front of 3 stakes and behind 1 but in reverse order, from right to left.

## TRIMMING OFF
### Trimming off ends of weavers

With the flat side of the sidecutters against the weaving, trim off the ends of the weavers left on both sides after joining (holding the cutters in this way produces a slanted cut that will lie level with the surface of the weaving). Note that it is essential that the cut end lies over a stick or stake otherwise the weaving will unravel. When making a round mat, for example, do not trim the ends until the border is completed. There is a certain amount of movement during weaving, and ends that are cut too short can come undone in the process. The ends can be coloured with felt-tip pens.

### Trimming off ends of border stakes

The ends of border stakes are trimmed off in a similar way to trimming off weavers. Note that the end must protrude slightly past the stake over which it is lying so that it doesn't unravel.

## STAKING UP

This is done after the base of a basket has been completed and is the process of inserting side stakes into the base.

Cut off the end of a stick close to the weaving, then insert a stake each side of it, pushing each down into the weaving as far as it will go – use a bodkin to open up the channel a little if necessary. Repeat for the other sticks, but only cut off the ends of 1 or 2 sticks at a time or your weaving will unravel. Soak the staked-up base in hot water for 5 to 10 minutes. Using the round-nosed pliers, squeeze each of the stakes as close to the edge of the weaving as possible, then bend them upwards, gathering them together.

## WORKING THE UPSETT

The first few rows of weaving after the staking up has been done and the new stakes have been gathered and tied together, are called the "upsett".

1 Turn the base on its side, with the bunch of stakes away from you, and insert 3 or 4 weavers – depending on whether you are going to work a three- or four-rod wale – into the channels in the weaving of the base, to the left of 3 (or 4) consecutive **stakes**. Use a bodkin to open up the weaving if necessary. Tie a short length of brightly coloured string around the stake immediately to the left of the lefthand weaver.

2 Keeping the base on its side, begin working a three- or four-rod wale (see above). Pull down on the weavers as you work in order to keep this first row of waling as close to the edge of the weaving of the base as possible. At the same time as you weave, spread out the stakes evenly around the base.

**3**

3 When the righthand weaver is in the space immediately to the left of the marked stake, work a three-rod or four-rod step-up (see above).

4 Turn the basket onto its base and put a weight inside to stop it moving around too much while you are weaving. The first few rows are critical to the final shape of the basket. If you want to achieve a cylindrical shape, make sure that you hold the stakes at 90° to the base, even **very slightly** outwards.

**4**

## INSERTING BYE-STAKES

Bye-stakes are generally inserted into the upsett waling on the righthand of a stake. They provide added strength and rigidity. Normally they are cut as long as the height (allowing for flow) of the sides of the basket.

## CONTROLLING THE SHAPE OF A BASKET

For sides that flow gently outwards, pull the stakes towards you a little as you weave, and vice versa if you want the sides to flow inwards. Untie the stakes only when you feel the sides are flowing in or out as you wish, but this should be by the end of the upsett (approximately 5 rows). Bear in mind that it is you who controls the shape of the basket, by controlling the stakes with your hands and the weaving — shaping the sides needs constant control and checking! Keep the stakes straight, keep the spaces between them even, and make sure each stake flows in or out at the same angle as the rest.

## CHECKING THAT THE TOP OF A BASKET IS LEVEL

Mark a spare length of cane at what looks to be the lowest point and use it to measure the height of the basket all round. If any points are too high, gently tap them down with a bodkin and retrim the bye-stakes if necessary.

## VARNISHING

Varnishing a cane basket serves two purposes: to provide a protective layer which helps to repel dirt, and to enhance and prolong the colour of dyed cane. Take care not to apply the varnish too thickly — it must be carefully brushed in or else it will "run" between the strands and look like glue. Always do the varnishing in a well-ventilated room. Clean brushes thoroughly in white spirit after use.

# Placemat

This simple project is an excellent one to do when you are beginning basketry. The technique used is similar to that used for making the bases of the Cylindrical Basket and the Shopping Basket.

## You will need

◊ The following sizes of cane:
No. 11 for the sticks
No. 5 for weaving (pairing)
No. 8 for the border stakes
◊ Suitable dye in 2 colours
◊ Mordant
◊ Dyeing equipment (see page 7)
◊ Sidecutters
◊ Tape-measure
◊ Bodkin
◊ Large washing-up bowl and warm to hot water
◊ Satin finish polyurethane or acrylic varnish
◊ Paintbrush
◊ White spirit

## Techniques used

☞ Dyeing Cane
☞ Cutting Cane
☞ Making the Slath
☞ Tying in the Slath
☞ Pairing
☞ Joining in a New Weaver in Pairing
☞ Completing Pairing
☞ Trimming off
☞ Varnishing
See pages 6 to 13

1 *Dye* most of the No. 5 cane in 2 colours. *Cut* 8 sticks, each 10¼in/26cm long, from the No. 11 cane. Soak the sticks in the water for 5 to 10 minutes to soften them.

2 *Make a slath*, 4 through 4, with the sticks. Soak the slath and the No. 5 cane in the water for 5 to 10 minutes to soften them.

3 Take a length of undyed No. 5 cane. *Tie in the slath* with 3 rows of *pairing*. Open out the sticks into pairs and work 2 rows, then open out the sticks into singles and work 2 rows.

4 You will now have worked 7 rows of pairing. Your sticks should be evenly spaced. Change from natural to coloured weavers by *joining in* 2 lengths of dyed No. 5 cane.

5 Continue pairing, keeping the sticks evenly spaced. Remember, too, that the mat will need to lie flat on a table, so keep checking that the sticks remain level.

6 Continue pairing for 15 rows, then *complete the pairing.* Dampen the mat from time to time.

7 Cut 16 border stakes from the No. 8 cane, each 13½in/34cm long. With the right side of the mat facing, cut off the end of a stick close to the weaving — the side facing you as you work — then insert a border stake to the lefthand side of the stick, pushing it down into the weaving to where the dyed weaving begins. If necessary, use the bodkin to open up the weaving a little to make inserting the stake easier. Insert the remaining border stakes in the same way, but cut off only 1 or 2 sticks at a time, or your weaving will unravel.

8 Soak the border stakes. With the right side facing work the first stage of the border, carefully bend a stake down to the right and weave it in front of the next stake, behind the next and back to the front.

9 Continue this process with each border stake. The last few border stakes need to be threaded through the stakes already worked. Be careful to maintain the same sequence by looking closely at the pattern created by the border so far.

10 To complete the border, work the end of each stake in front of the stake to the right of it (imagine the stake is still standing upright) and over the end of the stake sticking out to the right. Thread it through to the back, just to the left of the second stake along to the right, between the last row of the coloured weaving and the border. The end will now lie behind this second stake to the right. Repeat with every stake, maintaining the pattern when working the last 2 stakes.

11 *Trim off* the ends of the weavers left on both sides of the mat after joining. With the wrong side of the mat facing, trim off the ends of the border stakes in a similar way. Finally, give the mat a coat of *varnish.*

# Tablemat

This is a slightly larger and thicker mat than the Placemat in the previous project and introduces a new weave. You can use this mat as a placemat or to protect the table under hot dishes. The main weave — a three-rod wale — produces a striking, radiating pattern when worked in three colours over a number of stakes divisible by 3 — essential to achieve this pattern.

**You will need**

◊ The following sizes of cane:

No. 14 for the sticks
No. 5 for weaving (pairing and waling)
No. 11 for the border stakes

◊ Suitable dye in 2 colours
◊ Mordant
◊ Dyeing equipment (see page 7)
◊ Sidecutters
◊ Tape-measure
◊ Bodkin
◊ Large washing-up bowl with warm to hot water
◊ Satin finish polyurethane or acrylic varnish
◊ Paintbrush
◊ White spirit

**Techniques used**

☞ Dyeing Cane
☞ Cutting Cane
☞ Making the Slath ·
☞ Tying in the Slath
☞ Pairing
☞ Joining in a New Weaver in Pairing
☞ Three-rod Wale
☞ Working a Step-up in a Three-rod Wale
☞ Joining in a Three-rod Wale
☞ Completing a Three-rod Wale
☞ Trimming off
☞ Varnishing
See pages 6 to 13

1 *Dye* just under ⅓ of the No. 5 cane in one of the colours and the same amount in the other colour. *Cut* 10 sticks, each 14¼in/36cm long, from the No. 14 cane and soak them. Pierce 5 of them through the centre with the bodkin.

2 *Make a slath*, threading 5 sticks through 5 sticks. Soak the slath and the undyed No. 5 cane for 5 to 10 minutes to soften them. *Tie in the slath* with 2 rows of *pairing*, using a length of undyed No. 5 cane.

3 On the third row, open out the sticks to give 3 groups of sticks each opened out as follows: a pair on the left, a single in the middle and a pair on the right.

4 *Complete the pairing* at the end of the next row — 4 rows in total.

5 On the righthand side of a pair of sticks, insert the bodkin to open up a channel in the weaving.

6 Cut an extra stick, 6in/15cm long, from the No. 14 cane and insert it into the channel you have made, pushing it down as far as it will go. This gives a total of 21 sticks – a number divisible by 3, which is necessary in order for the 3-colour pattern to work. Soak some of the undyed and the dyed No. 5 cane.

7 Spread out the sticks into singles. Lay 3 No. 5 weavers – 1 natural and 1 of each dyed colour into 3 consecutive spaces. Tie a marker onto the stake to the left of the lefthand weaver. Don't begin waling near the extra stick inserted in step 6.

8 Begin a *three-rod wale*. At the same time as you weave open out the sticks into singles.

9 When working a wale in cane, it is usual to work a *step-up* at the end of every row. This means that each row is completed, preventing the weave spiralling. Now work a step-up.

10 Begin the second row as before, starting with the lefthand weaver. Continue, working a step-up at the end of each row. When you need to, *join in* new cane but **don't** join at or near a step-up. Work 20 rows of three-rod waling altogether. Work a step-up at the end of the last row, then *complete the three-rod wale*.

11 Cut 21 border stakes from the No. 11 cane, each 13½in/34cm long. With the wrong side of the mat facing, use the sidecutters to cut off the end of a stick close to the weaving. Insert a border stake into the channel in the weaving to the right of the stick (use the bodkin to open this up a little if necessary), pushing the stake down to where the 3-rod wale started. Insert the remaining border stakes in the same way, but only cut off 1 or 2 sticks at a time, or your weaving will unravel.

12 Soak the border stakes. With the right side facing work the first stage of the border, carefully bend a stake down to the right and weave it in front of the next stake, behind the next and back to the front.

13 Continue this process with each border stake. The last few border stakes need to be threaded through the stakes already worked. Be careful to maintain the same sequence by looking closely at the pattern created by the border so far.

14 To complete the border, work the end of each stake in front of the stake to the right of it (imagine the stake is still standing upright) and over the end of the stake sticking out to the right. Thread it through to the back, just to the left of the second stake along to the right, between the last row of the coloured weaving and the border. The end will now lie behind this second stake to the right. Repeat with every stake, maintaining the pattern when working the last 2 stakes.

15 *Trim off* the ends of the weavers left on both sides of the mat after joining.

16 *Trim the ends* of the border stakes in a similar way. Take care not to cut the ends too short to the weaving will unravel. Finally, *varnish* the mat to protect it.

# Cylindrical Basket

A versatile basket that could be equally useful as a container for a pot plant or for waste paper. As well as introducing new skills, this project builds on those learned in the previous two projects and combines all the techniques learned so far. If you like, you can easily plot alternative coloured patterns on graph paper.

## You will need

◊ The following sizes of cane:

No. 14 for the sticks
No. 5 for weaving (pairing and waling)
No. 8 for the stakes and bye-stakes

◊ Suitable dye in 4 colours: dark brown, dusky pink, dark yellow and orange
◊ Mordant
◊ Dyeing equipment (see page 7)
◊ Sidecutters
◊ Tape-measure
◊ Bodkin
◊ Round-nosed pliers
◊ String
◊ Weight
◊ Large washing-up bowl and warm to hot water
◊ Satin finish polyurethane or acrylic varnish
◊ Paintbrush
◊ White spirit
◊ Graph paper and coloured pencils

## Techniques used

☞ Dyeing Cane
☞ Cutting Cane
☞ Making the Slath
☞ Tying in the Slath
☞ Pairing
☞ Joining in a New Weaver in Pairing
☞ Completing Pairing
☞ Three-rod waling
☞ Working a Step-up in a Three-rod Wale
☞ Joining in a Three-rod Wale
☞ Staking up
☞ Working the Upsett
☞ Completing Waling
☞ Trimming off
☞ Checking that the Top of a Basket is Level
☞ Varnishing
See pages 6 to 13

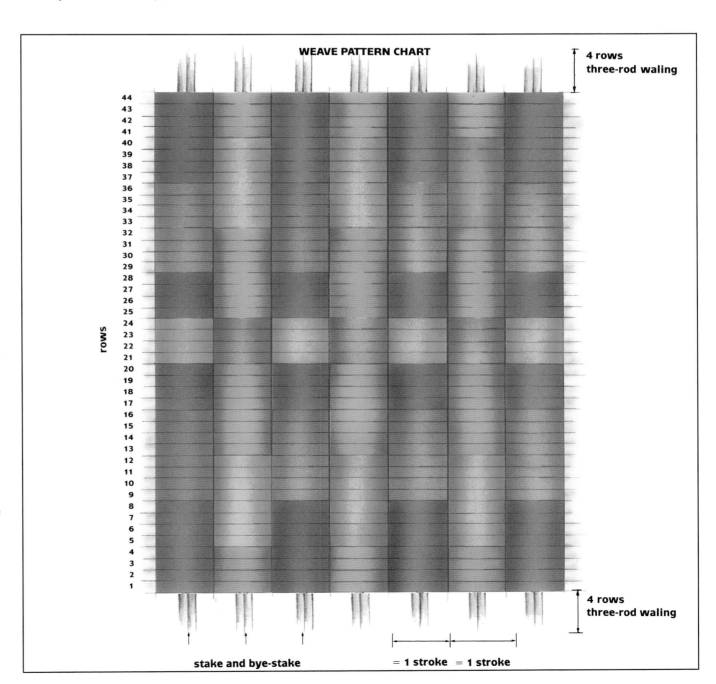

**WEAVE PATTERN CHART**

4 rows
three-rod waling

rows

4 rows
three-rod waling

stake and bye-stake    = 1 stroke  = 1 stroke

1 *Dye* most of the No. 5 cane in the 4 colours. *Cut* 8 sticks, each 12½in/32cm long, from the No. 14 cane. Soak the sticks in the water for 5 to 10 minutes to soften them. *Make a 4-through-4 slath* with the sticks. Soak the slath and some undyed No. 5 cane in the water. Take a length of No. 5 cane and *tie in the slath* with 2 rows of *pairing*. On the 3rd row, open out the sticks to pairs.

2 Work 2 rows with the sticks in pairs, then open out the sticks to singles and continue pairing until the diameter is about 9in/23cm. At the same time, while weaving, gently push the sticks away from you to create a **very slightly** domed shape — like a shallow saucer. *Complete the pairing.*

3 Cut 32 stakes, each 24½in/62cm long, from the No. 8 cane. *Stake up* the base by inserting a stake on either side of each base stick, pushing each one down as far as it will go, using the bodkin, if necessary, to open a channel in the weaving. Then soak the staked-up base and some undyed No. 5 cane in water for 5–10 minutes.

4 Using the round-nosed pliers, squeeze each of the stakes as close to the edge of the base weaving as possible, then carefully bend them upwards, gathering them together in your hand as you do them.

5 Cut a length of string and tie up the stakes in a bunch about 12in/30cm above the base, keeping the bunch located centrally over the base. *Start the upsett*, with 3 soaked undyed No. 5 cane weavers. After the first row, turn the basket onto its base and put the weight on it, to anchor it down. Work a total of 5 rows of *three-rod waling* for the *upsett*, then *complete the waling* and untie the stakes.

7 Now begin weaving the sides. Lay 1 dark brown No. 5 cane weaver in 1 space and 1 dusky pink No. 5 cane weaver in the next space and pair for 4 rows.

8 At the end of the 4th row *join in* a dark yellow No. 5 cane weaver in place of the dusky pink one and continue pairing for 4 more rows.

6 Cut 32 bye-stakes, each 11½in/29cm long, from the No. 8 cane. *Insert a bye-stake* into the waling to the righthand side of every stake.

9 Join in an orange No. 5 cane weaver in place of the brown one and continue weaving in the same way, changing the colours of the weavers as indicated on the chart, until you have worked 44 rows of pairing altogether. As you weave, *trim off* the ends of the weavers on the inside of the basket as you go, but leave the ends on the outside as they are. Also, constantly *check the shape of the basket*. If it is beginning to flow inwards or outwards it is worth undoing a few rows of weaving at this stage, to correct the shape, rather than being dissatisfied with the end result.

10 Lay 3 undyed No. 5 cane weavers in 3 consecutive spaces and mark the step-up by tying a short length of string to the stake immediately to the left of the lefthand weaver. Begin a three-rod wale.

11 Remembering to work a *step-up* at the end of each row, work 4 rows.

12 *Complete the waling*. Remove the marker.

13 With the flat side of the sidecutters pressing down slightly on the weaving, cut off the remaining ends of the bye-stakes. *Check that the top of the basket is level* — trimming bye-stakes, if necessary. Soak the stakes well in the water.

right and weave it in front of 2 stakes and behind 1 and so on until you get to the last 2 stakes.

14 Next, work the first stage of the border. Bring each upright stake down to the right and weave it in front of 2 upright stakes and behind 1 upright stake. Leave the stake on the inside of the basket. Take the next stake to the

15 To work the last 2 upright stakes, first bring the lefthand stake down to the right in front of the 1 remaining upright stake and in front of and under the stake to the right, to lie behind the second stake that was brought down. Finally bring the last upright stake down in front of and under the 2 stakes to its right to lie behind the third stake that was brought down. All ends should now be on the inside of the basket.

x  y  a  b  c  d

x  y  a  b  c  d

**inside of basket**

A  B

A  B

16 To work the second stage of the border, bring each stake back to the outside by bringing each stake end over the 2 stake ends to its right, and then to the outside by threading it between the side weaving and the border.

17 When only 2 stakes **x** and **y** remain on the inside, take the lefthand stake, **x**, and work it behind two stakes (**b** and **c** – imagine them still upright), over the last stake remaining on the inside – **y** – and then to the outside between the side weaving and the border. Finally, take the last stake **y** behind two stakes (**c** and **d** – imagine them upright), over **a** and **b** (imagine them still on the inside) and thread **y** to the outside between the border (ie under **c** and **d** and the side weaving).

18 To work the final stage of the border, take each stake to the inside of the basket again by taking each one in front of the 2 stakes immediately to the right of it (imagine the stakes standing upright), over the stake sticking out immediately to its right, then through to the back between the weaving and the border to lie behind the third stake along to the right.

19 When you are certain that the border is correct, trim off the ends of the border stakes. It is better to trim these ends so that they are a fraction too long rather than cut them too short. Trim off the ends of the weavers on the outside of the basket. *Varnish* the basket inside and out.

# Shopping Basket

It would be a shame to only carry potatoes in this wonderfully colourful basket —
a few red peppers, a yellow melon, green apples and some aubergines would be
much more in keeping with its cheerful colours.

1 *Dye* most of the No. 5 cane in the 4 colours. *Cut* 9 sticks 12½in/32cm long, from the No. 14 cane. Soak the sticks in the water for 5 to 10 minutes to soften them.

2 *Make a five through four slath* with the sticks, threading 5 sticks through 4. Soak the slath and the undyed No. 5 cane in the water for 5 to 10 minutes to soften them.

3 Take a length of No. 5 cane and *tie in the slath* with 2 rows of *pairing*. On the third row begin opening out the sticks as follows: the groups of 4 into pairs and the groups of 5 into a pair, a single and a pair. NB Keep the central, single, sticks in the groups of 5 straight.

4 On the 5th row, open out the sticks to singles. Make certain that you keep the 2 singles of step 2 straight. This is important as later they act as guides for the positioning of the handle. Continue pairing until the diameter is about 8¾in/22cm. As you work, gently push the sticks away from you to create a **very slightly** domed shape, like a shallow saucer. *Complete the pairing.* The base will be slightly oval in shape due to the number of sticks used in the slath. Cut 36 stakes 23½in/60cm long, from No. 11 cane.

5 *Stake up the base* by inserting a stake either side of each base stick, pushing each one down as far as it will go, using the bodkin, if necessary, to open up the space in the weaving. Soak the staked-up base in hot water for 5 to 10 minutes. Using the round-nosed pliers, squeeze each of the stakes as close to the edge of the weaving as possible, then carefully bend them upwards, gathering them together in your hand as you squeeze each stake.

6 Cut a length of string and tie up the stakes in a bunch about 12in/30cm above the base. Insert 4 soaked, undyed No. 8 weavers into the base, weaving to the left of 4 consecutive stakes. Remember to mark the stake to the left of the lefthand weaver. Begin *working the upsett* using a *four-rod wale*. Work a *four-rod step-up* at the end of each row.

7 After the first row turn the basket onto its base, put a weight on its base, and pull the stakes towards you as you weave so that the sides of the basket begin to flow gently outwards. At the end of the third row untie the stakes — they should now be leaning outwards at the angle you want the sides of the finished basket to be. *Complete the four-rod wale* at the end of the fifth row.

8 Cut 36 bye-stakes 8¾in/22cm long, from No. 11 cane. Insert 1 to the right of each stake.

9 Lay in 3 soaked No. 5 weavers in green, blue and red, in 3 consecutive spaces, but not directly above where the four-rod wale ended.

Begin working a *three-rod wale*, marking the stake to the left of the lefthand weaver to mark the step-up.

stake and bye-stake

**4 rows four-rod waling**

**three-rod waling for colour blocks**

= 1 stroke    = 1 stroke

**WEAVE PATTERN CHART**

**4 rows four-rod waling**

10 Work 5 rows, with a *step-up* at the end of each row. *Complete the waling.* Starting in a different place, lay in 3 new No. 5 weavers in consecutive spaces as follows: red where the green was, blue where the red was, yellow where the blue was. Mark where the new step-up will occur and remember to work one at the end of every row. At the end of the next 5 rows, complete this block of waling as before. Start the third block of waling in another place – remember to mark the step-up – and refer to the pattern chart to see which colour weaver is to go where.

11 When the third block of waling has been worked, make and insert the handle liners (the markers) by cutting 2 lengths of handle cane, each about 12in/30cm long, and use the craft knife to shave one end of each length to a two-sided point about 2–2½in/5–6.5cm long.

12 Look at the base of the basket and note where the oval is narrower across the middle. See where the central stick of the group of 5 sticks passed through the 4 in the slath and follow it out across the base of the basket (see the photo detail). Each end of this stick will carry 2 stakes. Push the handle liner down into the channel to one side of one of these stakes — the most central one — as far as it will go, to the bottom if possible. Find the corresponding stakes on the opposite side and insert the second handle liner. Check the positioning of the handle liners from above.

13 To emphasize the oval shape of the basket thread a long piece of strong string through the weaving from one side to the other, round the outside, back through and out the other side and tie the ends together tightly. The handle liners need to be opposite each other across the narrowest part of the oval as shown in the diagram. Check that the oval the string creates is the shape you desire — but not too extreme — adjusting the string now if necessary.

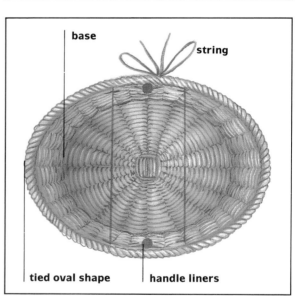

base
string

tied oval shape    handle liners

14 Continue working the blocks of three-rod wale as before, treating the handle liner and stake it is next to as one, referring to the chart. Remember to *control the shape of the basket* all the time and to begin each block of colour pattern in a different place and to mark and *work the step-up*. After the sixth and last colour block, complete the three-rod waling. Lay in 4 soaked, undyed No. 8 weavers into 4 consecutive spaces.

15 Work 4 rows of four-rod waling, working a four-rod step-up at the end of each row. Complete the four-rod waling.

**16**

16 *Trim off* the bye-stakes (take care not to cut the stakes) and *check that the top of the basket is level* – re-trimming bye-stakes if necessary. Soak the stakes well. Then, with the round-nosed pliers resting lightly on the side weaving, pinch each stake.

**17**

17 Cut a length of handle cane about 8in/ 20cm longer than the circumference of the top rim of the basket. This is to be the border core. Using the craft knife, shave down one side of one end of the border core for about 3½in/ 8cm. Hold the border core outside the top edge of the basket in front of a handle liner, and with the shaved end facing you. The rest of the border core should be lying to the right. Tie it to the handle liner with a piece of string.

**18**

18 Next, work the first stage of the border. Stake **a** is brought down to the right, in front of stakes **b** and **c**, over the core, then threaded under the core to lie behind stake **d**. Stake **b** is then brought down to the right, in front of **c** and **d**, over the core. It is then threaded under the core to lie behind stake **e**, and so on, until all the stakes are on the inside of the basket.

**19**

19 When you have gone almost all the way round, trim and shave the other end of the border core on the inside, to match up with the other end as closely as possible so that the 2 ends lie together as if one. Remove the string and re-tie, holding both ends together and to the handle liner and complete stage one of the border working over the joined border cane to secure it. Take care to maintain the pattern sequence.

**20**

20 The second stage of the border is worked by bringing each stake back up and over the core again, each stake following the path of the stake to its right. Take **a** and bring it back over the core again following, on the lefthand side, the path of **d**. Then thread it back to the inside again between the side weaving and the border. **a** will now be lying to the left of **d**, forming a pair. Repeat with **b** and then **c**, so that they form pairs with **e** and **f** respectively. Continue this process until all the strands are back to singles, coming out of consecutive spaces all round the basket.

**inside of basket**

**21** Finally, take all the ends to the outside by taking each strand to the right, behind a stake (imagine it upright), over the end immediately to its right, and thread it to the outside between the side weaving and the border, just before the next stake along, which it will rest against. So take **a** behind **i**, over **b**, under the border to the outside just before **ii**. Take all the ends to the outside in the same way.

**22** Check that the pattern sequence created by the border is correct and the tension is even, then trim off the ends of the border stakes and weavers. Leave the basket to dry.

**23** Cut a length of handle cane about 35–37in/90–95cm long to make the handle "bow". Using the craft knife, shave one end to a two-sided point 2–2½in/5–6.5cm long. Briefly soak the handle bow to prevent it being brittle. Remove 1 handle liner and push the pointed end of the handle bow into the same channel in the weaving **with the cut side inwards**. Carefully bend the handle bow over the top of the basket and measure how long it needs to be. Allow for it to curve – about 5½–6in/14–15cm above the border at the top of

the curve – and to go right down into the weaving on the other side. Cut it to the right length and shave the end to a point as for the other end. Remove the other handle liner and push the end of the handle bow firmly down into the channel in the weaving. Adjust the shape of the handle until you have a good, even curve.

**24** The handle is now pegged to secure it. Cut 2 short lengths of No. 11 cane. Push the bodkin right through the handle between the second and third rows of the four-rod wale.

**25** Quickly insert 1 of the pieces of No. 11 cane into the hole and, keeping in mind the purpose of the peg, trim off the ends by laying the flat side of the sidecutters against the weaving when cutting. Repeat this on the other side.

**26** To cover the handle bow, take 4 or 5 strands of the dyed No. 5 cane, 5 times the length of the handle and thread them through the weaving to the left of the handle between the three- and four-rod waling. Pull the ends through to the inside until you have 1½ times the length of the handle. Take the ends on the outside of the basket diagonally up across the handle and, making sure the strands do not become twisted, wrap them around the handle 3 or 4 times, leaving equal-sized gaps between the "bands" of coloured cane.

*27* When you reach the other side, take the strands diagonally down across the handle and thread the ends through to the inside between the three- and four-rod waling as before. Both ends of the handle should look the same, with the diagonal band of cane going from top right to bottom left. Then bring the ends of the cane on the inside up and to the front keeping to the left of the handle bow. Wind them back over the handle, laying the new band of cane in the gap above the first. When you reach the other side, leave the strands on the inside. Repeat this procedure using the long strands of cane remaining on the inside of the opposite side.

*28* If after wrapping the handle there are still some small gaps — "grins" — take another strand of dyed No. 5 cane and wind it along the path where the grins are. The ends of this strand of cane lie with both groups of ends left on the inside from the previous stages. There may still be some very small grins on top of the handle, but it is best to leave these as the curve on the top of the handle bow is longer than that underneath.

*29* To bind each end of the handle, insert a length of No. 5 cane down to the right side of the handle bow. Bring it to the outside and wrap it clockwise around the handle 5 or 6 times, as tightly as possible. Thread the end back down through the binding, following the same diagonal as the cane wound round the handle and using a bodkin, if necessary, to create enough room to do this. Then pull the end down to tighten the binding, leaving it on the back of the handle. Repeat this on the opposite side of the basket.

*30* Using the sidecutters, carefully trim off the ends of the cane used to wrap and bind the handle so that they lie against the inside of the border and top rows of waling. *Varnish* the basket inside and out.

# CHAPTER 2
# USING CARDBOARD

## INTRODUCTION

Some of the best cardboard boxes to use are those that have been used to deliver cereal to shops and supermarkets. Crisp boxes can also be used, but are often made from low-quality cardboard that tends to tear easily and they will often have a perforated shape in one side to be pressed out so shops can display them for customers to serve themselves – this means that you will need more boxes. Large boxes that have been used for, say, packaging a shower unit or radiator are ideal.

If you ask at your corner shop, more often than not, they will keep a few suitable boxes aside for you to collect. Otherwise, some supermarkets have them near the checkouts for customers to use. Early morning is a good time to go as there is usually a good selection then. The two most important qualities to look for when selecting boxes are:

■ **size** the circumference must be sufficient to produce strips of the length required. The number of boxes you will need to collect to give the right number of strips will depend on the height of the boxes.

■ **type of cardboard** the cardboard must be corrugated, but with only a single layer of corrugations as those with a double layer are too stiff to weave with. If possible, especially for your first few baskets, choose boxes of a similar type in terms of thickness and malleability (as a rough guide, the cardboard should be no thicker than ⅛in/3mm). Ideally, boxes should be identical.

Once you have collected your boxes, open them up along the join, which will be in one of the corners. Flatten out each box and cut off the top and bottom flaps, leaving a large rectangle of cardboard.

Next, paint one (or both) sides of the cardboard. Large, bold, colourful, random designs often work well. Bear in mind that the sheets will be cut up and woven, mixing up all the elements of your original pattern in a completely random and unexpected way. As for the colours you choose, be inspired, for example, by the home for your basket.

## THE TECHNIQUES YOU NEED TO KNOW

The projects that follow have a number of techniques in common and these are explained below. The techniques used in any one project are listed beneath the materials, and references to them in the step-by-step instructions are printed in *italics*. Until you are familiar with the techniques it is best to read through the relevant sections below before starting a project, in order to produce the best results. There are valuable tips and clear explanations that, to avoid repetition, are not described in such detail in the projects.

### Preparing Cardboard Strips for Weaving

There are several important points to remember before you cut the prepared cardboard into strips:

◊ it is essential to cut *across* the corrugations as, otherwise, the strips will be virtually impossible to fold or bend

◊ measure and draw your strips very carefully to make them easier to work with and to produce a regular-shaped basket.

1 Using a ruler and a long straight edge, mark and rule the lines for the strips on the cardboard. Cut carefully along the lines with a pair of strong, sharp scissors, keeping the edges of the strips as straight as possible.

2 If there are any weak points in your strips, such as split corner creases, neatly "bandage" these using good-quality clear tape.

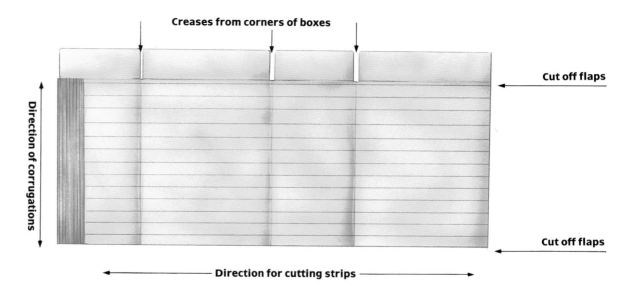

**Creases from corners of boxes**

**Cut off flaps**

**Cut off flaps**

**Direction of corrugations**

**Direction for cutting strips**

## Weaving a Square Base

The number of strips used will depend on the size of basket you are making, the width of the strips, and whether it is to be square or rectangular, so the numbers of strips given here are just an example.

1 To make a basket with a base which has 6 strips in each direction, take 4 strips of the required length and mark the centre of each. Form a cross with 2 strips in each direction and line up the marks. Weave them so that each strip goes over 1 strip and under the next.

2 Make sure the strips are pushed tightly together, and mark the centre with an "X". Now tightly fold back one strip – **a** – which lies underneath another strip – **y**.

3 Place a new strip – **z** – on top of the strip still lying flat – **b**. This must be close up against the edge of the adjacent strip **y**. Then fold back strip **b** over strip **z**.

4 Fold strip **a** back down over **z**. Think of this side you have just been working on as **side one** of the base.

5 Next, working on **side two**, tightly fold back strip **y**, which lies underneath strip **b**.

6 Lay a new strip – **c** – over strips **x** and **z**, close up to the edge of adjacent strip **b**. Fold strip **y** back down. There are now 3 strips in each direction. Add one strip each to **side three and four** to give 4 strips in each direction. Always make sure to fold tightly the relevant strips up and down when working as this keeps the weaving tight. Use pegs to keep the weaving tight.

7 Add a further strip to each side to give 6 strips in each direction. Tighten up the weaving. The base should be flat and square with no gaps between the strips. All strips must travel over one, under one. Peg each corner.

## Starting the Sides of a Basket

Note that the strips used for weaving the base will now be called the "stakes" and those for the sides "weavers".

1 Bend the stakes upwards. Place the end of a new strip between the 2 central stakes of one side, checking that the over 1, under 1 pattern is continued from the base up the sides. Fold the stake from the inside tightly down over the weaver to the outside and peg. Fold the outside stake tightly down over the weaver to the inside and peg.

2 Continue this folding and pegging procedure around all 4 sides of the basket. Be careful to maintain the inside and outside folding sequence around the corners, and peg the strips which fold to the outside. At the end of each row, overlap the ends of the weaver across 3 to 4 stakes (see the photo in step 3).

3 Begin the second row on another side. Place the weaver between 2 central stakes so that the 2nd weaver will work the opposite to the 1st weaver, so maintaining the over 1, under 1 pattern. Peg the strips which fold to the outside. Overlap ends as before.

4 Work the required number of rows, beginning each row on a different side to the previous one. Maintain the over 1, under 1 pattern and keep the tension tight so there are no gaps in the weaving.

## Stitching

1 Measure a length of thread which easily goes round the circumference of the basket, with a bit extra, and double it. Thread the needle so that you are using a double thickness of thread. Make a big knot about 2½in/6cm from the end of the thread.

2 Start with the knot on the outside and sew around the top row of the basket, using running stitch. Keep the stitching tight and at the end of the row tie off the ends very securely. NB: Make sure the ends of the stakes remain upright while sewing.

## Trimming off the Ends of the Stakes and Weavers

1 When trimming off the ends of the stakes, take care to cut them level with (or even fractionally below) the top edge of the last weaver.

2 Trim off the ends of the weavers left on the outside by pulling gently on the ends and carefully cutting as close to the edge of the stake as possible. The end of the weaver should then disappear behind the stake. Do the same on the inside.

## Joining Cardboard Strips

1 Peel away the unpainted layer and the corrugations, leaving only the top painted layer of paper to produce a flap about 2in/5cm long.

2 Glue the underside of the flap and stick it to the painted side of another strip. Use pegs to keep it in place until it is dry. If necessary, bandage the join with good-quality clear tape.

## Blanket Stitch

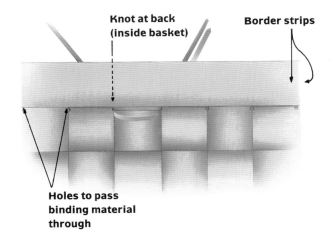

**Knot at back (inside basket)**

**Border strips**

**Holes to pass binding material through**

**Direction of binding material**

**Woven cardboard side of basket**

1 Measure a length of binding material about 3½ times the circumference of the basket and tie a loose knot about 6in/15cm from the end. Thread it through a hole (*not* at a corner) from back to front so the knot is left on the inside with the long length on the outside. Thread the binding material through the next hole along, from front to back, to form a horizontal stitch.

2 Next, bring the binding material up behind the border strips, over the top of the border and thread the end down, underneath the horizontal stitch. Tighten, and check that the vertical line of the stitch is lined up with the

vertical lines of the edges of the weaving stakes. Thread the end through the next hole along, and so on.

3 Work the last stitch to match the rest of the pattern — both ends should finish at the back. Undo the first knot, then tie both ends securely together under the border strips and trim the ends to about 1in/2cm.

## "Sandwich and Sew" Border

1 Cover the back of one strip with glue and, starting on the inside of the basket, on a different side from where the last row begins and ends and not at a corner. Stick the strip to the inside of the top row. Keep this strip level with the top of the basket, and make a sharp crease around the corners. Peg to secure. Join the strips neatly using the technique for *joining strips*. Then, beginning on another side, glue a second strip to the outside of the top row.

2 Using a bodkin, make holes at the top corners of each of the "squares" of the row just below the border strips. The border strips are now securely bound onto the basket using blanket stitch.

**Two strips of cardboard sandwiching sides of basket**

**Binding material**

**Woven cardboard side of basket**

## Varnishing

Give the finished basket a thin coat of varnish inside and out, brushing well into the edges of the strips. Make sure there are no drips or runs. Always do your varnishing in a well-ventilated area and clean your brushes thoroughly in white spirit after use.

# Waste-paper Basket

This basket is made from recycled cardboard boxes. The boxes have been painted with a bold, colourful pattern, but you may prefer to choose colours that co-ordinate with a room in your home or workplace. It can be a good way in which to use up paint left-over from decorating.

1 *Prepare* and paint the cardboard boxes.

**You will need**
◊ 2 to 3 large cardboard boxes
◊ Household vinyl or PVA-type paint
◊ Paintbrushes
◊ 3ft/1m ruler
◊ Pencil
◊ Scissors
◊ Good quality clear adhesive tape
◊ At least 12 hinged clothes-pegs
◊ Strong thread
◊ Sharp needle with large eye
◊ Glue stick
◊ Bodkin or awl
◊ Brightly coloured polypropylene string
◊ Satin finish polyurethane or acrylic varnish
◊ Paintbrush
◊ White spirit

**Techniques used**
☞ Preparing Cardboard Strips for Weaving
☞ Weaving a Square Base
☞ Starting the Sides of a Basket
☞ Trimming the Ends of Stakes and Weavers
☞ Joining Cardboard Strips
☞ Stitching
☞ Sandwich and Sew Border
☞ Blanket Stitch
☞ Varnishing
See pages 30 to 33

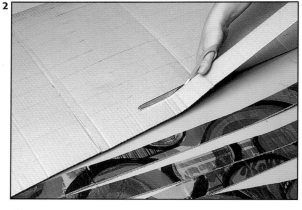

2 Mark out 24 1½in-/4cm-wide strips 47¼in/120cm long on the wrong side of the prepared cardboard (this gives you 3 spare strips). Remember to cut *across* the corrugations and not along them.

4 Work 7 rows, beginning each row on a different side to the previous one. Maintain the over 1, under 1 pattern and keep the tension tight so there are no gaps between the weaving. Peg to secure.

3 Weave the base of the basket following the instructions for *weaving a square base*. When you have 6 strips in each direction peg the corners. Then begin *weaving the sides of the basket*, as described on page 32.

5 Using doubled strong thread, work running *stitch* along the top row to secure the weaving. The stakes should be upright at this point. *Trim off the ends* of the stakes and weavers.

6 Work a *sandwich and sew border*, but don't begin or end it where you began and ended the last row of the side weaving.

7 Glue one border strip to the inside of the top row, and, starting on another side again, glue the 2nd border strip to the outside of the top row. Overlap the ends of each strip using the technique for *joining cardboard strips*. Peg in place.

8 Make holes through which the binding material can pass.

9 Measure a length of binding material (polypropylene string) 3½ times the circumference of the basket. Bind the border using *blanket stitch*. *Varnish* the basket inside and out.

# Shopping Basket

The method used here is similar to that used for the Waste-paper Basket, except that the Shopping Basket is rectangular instead of square.

## You will need

◊ 2 to 3 large cardboard boxes
◊ Household vinyl or PVA-type paint in red, yellow, green, mid-blue and dark blue
◊ Paintbrushes
◊ 3ft/1m ruler
◊ Pencil
◊ Scissors
◊ Good quality clear adhesive tape
◊ At least 20 hinged clothes-pegs
◊ Strong thread
◊ Sharp needle with large eye
◊ Glue stick
◊ Bodkin or awl
◊ Brightly coloured polypropylene string or similar
◊ Hole-making tool that will make large holes
◊ 4 ³⁄₈in/10mm brass eyelets and punch and die kit
◊ Hammer
◊ 1 ½yd/91cm of ³⁄₈in-/10mm-diameter rope
◊ Satin finish polyurethane or acrylic varnish
◊ Paintbrush
◊ White spirit

## Techniques used

☞ Preparing Cardboard Strips for Weaving
☞ Starting the Sides of a Basket
☞ Joining Cardboard Strips
☞ Trimming off the Ends of Stakes and Weavers
☞ Stitching
☞ Sandwich and Sew Border
☞ Blanket Stitch
☞ Varnishing
See pages 30 to 33

1 *Prepare* the cardboard boxes, then paint in different plain colours – red, yellow, green, mid-blue and dark blue. Leave to dry.

2 On the unpainted side of the prepared cardboard mark and cut 1½in-/4cm-wide strips of the following lengths:

3 strips 43¼in/110cm long – 1 x mid-blue, 1 x dark blue, 1 x green
9 strips 31½in/80cm long – 3 x dark blue, 4 x green, 2 x mid-blue
8 strips 47¼in/120cm long – 4 x red, 3 x yellow, 1 x dark blue
(plus 2 extra in case any strips break)
Remember to cut *across* the corrugations, not along them.

3 Mark the centre on the three 43¼in/110cm strips and lay them side by side, crosswise (mid-blue/dark blue/green. Take one of the 31½in/80cm strips (dark blue) and weave it through the 3 crosswise strips at the marked centre points, going over the first, under the second, over the third. Mark the centre point.

4 Weave the base by working 4 of the 31½in/80cm strips to the left of the central strip (green, mid-blue, green, dark blue). Make sure all strips travel over 1, under 1.

5 Repeat this last step to the right of the central strip – keep colours in the same order as step 4 – and peg the corners. You should now have a rectangle of weaving three 43¼in/110cm strips by nine 31½in/80cm strips, with the marked strip in the centre.

6 Take a yellow strip, and starting at a central point on a *long* edge, begin *weaving the sides of the basket* using the 47¼in/120cm strips. At the end of the row overlap the ends of the weaver across 3–4 stakes.

7 Using a red strip, begin the second row on the opposite long side.

8 Work 6 rows in this way, beginning each row on an opposite side to the one just worked (but always on a long side). *Stitch* along the top row to secure the weaving, using running stitch and a double strand of strong thread. *Trim off the ends* of the stakes and the weavers.

9 Begin a *sandwich and sew* border by glueing one of the dark blue 47¼in/120cm border strips to the inside of the top row of the basket and the other red one to the outside and peg in place, *joining* the ends neatly. Leave to dry.

10 Make holes for the binding material to pass through. Measure a length of binding material 3½ times the circumference of the basket. Work *blanket stitch* to bind the border strips.

11 Using the hole-making tool or a large bodkin, make 2 clean holes that the brass eyelets will fit into on each side of the basket. These should be in the first row below the border strip, in the third "square" in from each corner, leaving 3 squares between each hole.

12 Insert and fix the eyelets into each hole following the manufacturer's instructions.

13 *Varnish* the basket inside and outside. Cut the rope for the handles in half and, if necessary, tape the ends to prevent them fraying. Pass them through the eyelets to the inside of the basket and tie knots in each end.

# Square Basket with Lid

You could easily imagine Aladdin hiding his lamp in this basket, but more probably his jewels and other precious things. This is a basket in which to keep love letters, necklaces, marbles and other special things; to stow them away out of sight and yet within easy access when the impulse to see them strikes.

## You will need

◊ 2 to 3 large cardboard boxes
◊ Wax crayons
◊ Household vinyl or PVA-type paint, thinned down with water
◊ Paintbrush
◊ 3ft/1m ruler
◊ Pencil
◊ Scissors
◊ Good quality clear adhesive tape
◊ At least 20 hinged clothes-pegs
◊ Strong thread
◊ Sharp needle with large eye
◊ Glue stick
◊ Bodkin or awl
◊ Polypropylene string
◊ Strong quick drying glue
◊ Satin finish polyurethane or acrylic varnish
◊ Paintbrush
◊ White spirit

## Techniques used

☞ Preparing Cardboard Strips for Weaving
☞ Joining Cardboard Strips
☞ Weaving a Square Base
☞ Starting the Sides of a Basket
☞ Trimming off the Ends of the Stakes and Weavers
☞ Stitching
☞ Sandwich and Sew Border
☞ Blanket Stitch
☞ Varnishing
See pages 30 to 33

1 *Prepare* the cardboard boxes, then draw a random pattern over the plain side with the wax crayons and paint over the top with the thinned paint. Leave to dry.

3 Begin *weaving the sides of the basket* at the centre of one edge of the base, using the 43¼in/110cm strips. Begin the second row of weaving on a different side.

2 On the unpainted side of the cardboard, mark out, rule and cut strips 1¼in/3cm wide to give the following lengths:

### For the basket

8 strips 43¼in/110cm long (for the weavers and 2 border strips)
16 strips 31½in/8cm long (for the stakes)

### For the lid

20 strips 12in/30cm long (for the weaving and border strips)
PLUS:
1 very long strip 118in/300cm long by ⅝in/1.5cm wide which will be used to form a ledge for the lid to sit on
A square of painted card 12 x 12in/30 x 30cm

Remember to cut the strips across the corrugations, not along them. *Weave a base* 8 strips by 8 strips using the 16 31½in/80cm strips.

4 Weave a total of 6 rows beginning each on a different side. *Stitch* along the top row with strong thread to secure the weaving, then *trim off the ends* of the stakes and the weavers.

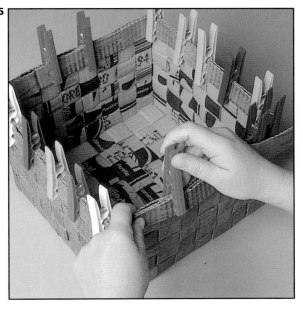

5 Using the remaining 2 43¼in/110cm strips work the first stage of a *sandwich and sew border*.

6 Measure a length of binding material 3½ times the circumference of the basket. Make holes under the border for this to pass through. Bind the border using *blanket stitch*.

7 Using the strong, quick-drying glue, stick the very long, narrow strip to the inner border strip, positioning it so that the bottom edge is level with the bottom edge of the border strip. The strip should go round the box 3 times to form a ledge 3 layers – about ⅜in/1cm – thick.

8 Working with the 12in/30cm long strips, weave the lid 8 strips by 8 strips in the same way as the base of the basket. Using strong thread stitch along the last rows of weaving, working slightly towards the inside edge of this row, to secure the weaving. *Trim off the ends* of the strips to leave a neat square of weaving.

9 Place the lid on the box and, very carefully, mark and trim the edges so that the lid will drop neatly into the basket and rest on the ledge. Make marks on the underside of the lid and on the corresponding inner side of the basket, so that you know which way round it fits best at a later stage.

10 Lay the lid, painted side up, on the unpainted side of the cardboard square and draw round the lid and cut out the square. Mark the unpainted side of the cardboard square to correspond with the marks on the lid and inside of the box.

11 Glue the unpainted side of the lid and the unpainted side of the cardboard square and stick them together, matching up the marked sides and the edges. Peg the two pieces together. Mark the lid again to correspond with the mark on the inner side of the basket. Weigh down the lid and leave to dry overnight.

12 Begin a *sandwich and sew* border by glueing the 4 remaining strips along the outer edges of the painted side of the lid, lining up the inner edge of the strips with the inner edge of the last weaver. Overlap the strips at the corners (as for *joining*) to avoid bulk. Peg in place, leave to dry, then trim off the excess, following the line of the edge of the lid.

13 Measure a length of binding material 3½ times the circumference and bind the border strips to the lid using *blanket stitch*.

14 Using a bodkin or awl, pierce a hole through the centre of the lid. Thread through a loop of the binding material and knot it underneath to make a handle. *Varnish* the basket and lid inside and out.

# USING RAFFIA

## INTRODUCTION

Natural, as opposed to synthetic, raffia comes in two qualities: unprepared and prepared. Unprepared raffia comes in hanks of varying sizes, sold by weight, ranging from about 3lb/1½kg to 6lb/3kg. As the name suggests, the hank is a mixed bundle of raffia in strands of varying lengths, thicknesses and quality, but is ideal for making the core bundle of coiled basketry projects.

For the stitching and wrapping, use prepared raffia which is the same material as unprepared raffia, except that the material has been selected to give more regular strands and comes in smaller bundles of 1½oz/40g.

Natural, unprepared raffia has a neutral, creamy colour, similar to cane. Raffia takes dye well, and prepared raffia can be bought ready-dyed.

## THE TECHNIQUES YOU NEED TO KNOW TO MAKE THE PROJECTS

The projects in this chapter have certain techniques in common and these are explained below. In the projects the techniques used are listed below the materials and references to them in the step-by-step instructions are printed in italics. Until you are familiar with these techniques, it is best to read through the relevant sections below before starting the project. You will find useful tips and clear explanations of the techniques here that will help you achieve good results and, to avoid repetition, these are not described in detail in the projects.

### Making the Core

Extract 10 or 12 strands of natural, unprepared raffia from a hank.

### The Stitching Material

Select a good strand from a bundle of prepared raffia. Any strands that are too frayed and ragged to use as stitching material can be used for core material. Thread the stitching material through a needle.

## Beginning a Round Base

1 Holding the core material in the middle, tie it in a single knot around your little finger. Take your finger out of the knot – this small loop will form the centre of the base. See Diagram A.

2 With the knot at the top, bring all the ends of the core to the lefthand side of the loop. Hold one end of the stitching material tightly in with the core bundle. Working anticlockwise, wrap around the loop with the stitching material working down into the hole in the middle. This is important for when you begin stitching.

3 When you reach the knot, continue wrapping around the loop for a second round, but this time incorporate the core.

4 When you reach the knot again, instead of taking the needle down through the middle of the loop, begin to stitch by taking the needle down through the coil (row), below. Imagine that each stitch is catching 6–8 strands of the core from the row below. Work the stitches quite closely together so that you cover the core. Note that the side facing you, into which you stitch down, is the right side.

**Diagram A**

## Joining in New Stitching Material

With the wrong side of the mat facing, thread the new strand under the previous stitching for about ½in/1cm (about 4 to 5 stitches), leaving an end of about ¾in/2cm sticking out. Turn the mat over so the right side is facing and continue stitching with the new strand as before, incorporating the remaining length of the old stitching material into the core. When working with several colours you can carry the different coloured strands, threaded onto a needle, in with the core bundle, picking up and dropping each colour as required by the design.

## Joining in New Core Material

When the core begins to feel a bit thin, simply push more strands into the existing core until it feels the same thickness as before. This is done by folding, say, 4 strands in half, then pushing the folded ends into the centre of the core and continuing to stitch as before.

# Coiled Mat

Baskets made in a similar way to this mat can be found in many countries around the world and have existed in more or less this form for many hundreds of years. The swirling pattern on this mat is loosely based on that of some coiled baskets from Botswana. You can use this mat to protect surfaces from hot dishes; make half a dozen and use them as place-mats, or hang a single mat on the wall as a decoration.

## You will need
◊ The following amounts and types of raffia:

small hank natural, dry unprepared raffia, (about ½lb/¼kg is plenty)
1 to 2 bundles undyed prepared raffia
1 to 2 bundles black prepared raffia
1 to 2 bundles brown prepared raffia

◊ 3 sharp needles with large eyes
◊ Scissors

## Techniques used
☞ Making the Core
☞ The Stitching Material
☞ Beginning a Round Base
☞ Joining in New Stitching Material
☞ Joining in New Core Material
See pages 41 to 42

1 Extract 10–12 strands from the natural, unprepared raffia to *make the core*. Select a good strand from a bundle of the undyed prepared raffia for the *stitching material* and *begin working a round base*.

2 When you have worked about 2 rows of stitching, thread a second needle with a strand of the black raffia and *join it* in, remembering to incorporate the remaining length of the undyed stitching material into the core, with the needle left on the end. Stitch round the mat until you are about a third of the way round. By now the core will be getting a bit thin so you will need to *join in some more core material* – do this earlier, if necessary.

3 With the wrong side facing join in a strand of brown raffia, and continue stitching, carrying the black and natural stitching material in with the core, and work another third round the mat. The brown and black strands should now feel secure, so *trim off the ends* left on the wrong side.

4 Pick up the strand of undyed raffia from the core (you can tell which it is because it will have the needle on the end) and, incorporating the brown and black strands into the core, continue stitching as before until you are within 4 or 5 stitches of the beginning of the black stitching. Pick up the black strand and stitch with it as before, incorporating the undyed and brown strands into the core until they are needed again.

5 Continue stitching round the mat in this way, joining in more core and stitching material as necessary and following the chart for when to change colour. As you work, keep the mat flat by holding the core forming the next row exactly where you want it to lie and use the stitching to hold it in place. Imagine that if you cut the mat in half and held it at eye

level you would be able to draw a straight line through the centre of all the coils (see the diagram below). In order to make a good round mat, keep the thickness of the core bundle even.

6 When you have worked 8 rows of the colour pattern, begin the next colour block. As you stitch, trim out strands from the core so the coil gradually becomes thinner and shorter as you stitch round, eventually reducing to nothing. Aim to complete this process within the one colour block.

 **Eye level**

7 At the end you will be stitching over only 4 or 5 strands of core. Finish off the mat by threading the strand of stitching material back through the stitching for about 2in/5cm, and then carefully cut it off close to the stitching so it slips behind it.

# Coiled Basket

If you think that this small basket is perfect for nuts and sweets, you are right! This style of basket is often found in North Africa and the Middle East — the decorative pointed border is particularly reminiscent of coiled baskets from these areas.

**You will need**

◊ The following amounts and types of raffia:

small hank natural dry raffia, unprepared (about ½lb/¼kg is plenty)

1 to 2 bundles purple prepared raffia
1 to 2 bundles yellow prepared raffia
1 to 2 bundles pink prepared raffia

◊ 3 sharp needles with large eyes
◊ Scissors

**Techniques used**

☞ Making the Core
☞ The Stitching Material
☞ Beginning a Round Base
☞ Joining in New Stitching Material
☞ Joining in New Core Material
See pages 41 to 42

1 Extract 10–12 strands from the natural, unprepared raffia to *make the core*. Select a good strand from a bundle of the purple prepared raffia for the *stitching material* and *begin a round base*.

2 When you have worked 2 to 3 rows of stitching, start following the pattern chart above. *Join in* a strand of yellow prepared raffia and at 4 equidistant points, work 1 or 2 yellow stitches. Continue using purple for the rest of the stitching. Then join in a pink strand and, following the pattern chart, at 4 points half-way between the yellow stitches, work 1 or 2 pink stitches. On this same row work 4–6

yellow stitches above those of the previous row (see the detail of the pattern chart). As before, the remaining stitching is purple. Join in new stitching or core material where necessary carrying the other stitching strands in with the core bundle while they are not being used. *Trim off* the ends of the joined-in strands when you feel they are secure.

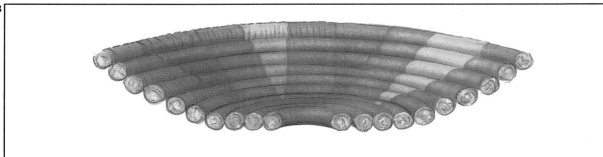

$3$ At the end of the third row of the pattern begin shaping the basket by holding the bundle of core material slightly up from — rather than directly in line with — the coil of the previous row (the photograph shows how to hold the basket and core material to achieve this). Imagine you are moulding the basket. The diagram shows how the curve is formed over several rows — it is a matter of holding the core material in the correct place and using each stitch to hold it there. When you begin shaping the basket, gradually increase the thickness of the core material until it is ³/₈– ⁵/₈in/1–1.5cm in diameter when stitched.

$4$ Continue working round in an anticlockwise direction, following the pattern charts. You might find it helpful to thread up several needles in preparation as there are a number of colour changes involved. Control the shape all the time, looking at the basket from different angles as you work to check that it is developing as evenly as possible.

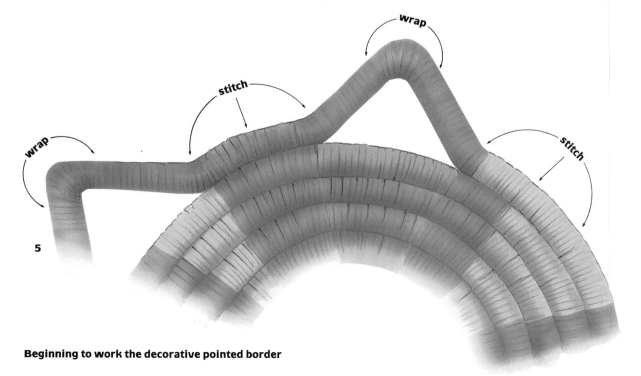

**Beginning to work the decorative pointed border**

$5$ At the end of the seventh row of the pattern (you should finish with a yellow block of stitching) begin working the decorative pointed border. Trim a few strands out of the core to produce a slightly thinner bundle, and continue stitching in yellow until just before you reach the pink block of the previous row. Pick up the purple strand, work 3 or 4 stitches and then wrap (not stitch) the core tightly until you have enough to form the point, bending the wrapped core into shape. Work a few stitches in purple just past the pink block, securing the point in position.

Pick up the pink strand and stitch until just before the yellow block of the previous row. Pick up the purple strand, work 2 stitches, then wrap (not stitch) the core to form a second point to match the first.

6 Secure it just past the yellow block of the previous row with 2 stitches.

Next pick up the yellow strand and stitch until just before the pink block. Continue in this way round the basket until you have wrapped the eighth and last point. Secure this point with 4 or 5 stitches.

Then trim away most of the core so that when you continue stitching, it tapers very quickly away to nothing. Stitch very securely over these ends, then thread the strand back through the stitching for a little way and trim off the end.

**6**

**Complete pattern and border**

## ACKNOWLEDGEMENTS

I would like to acknowledge the following people who have helped me either in becoming a basketmaker, or in the preparation of this book, or both: Jill Brownbill, one of my art teachers from school who encouraged me through idle teenage years and believed, I think, that I'd do something worthwhile one day.

Lois Walpole and Mary Butcher, two of my tutors at the (ex-) London College of Furniture (now London Guildhall University), both of whom taught me much of what I know about basketry. Lois's own work was not only an inspiration to me but also a revelation; Mary has opened many doors for me in terms of basketry as a subject to be explored historically and ethnographically.

Dick Speed of Technology Associates, Oxon, who put my name forward as an author for this book.

The Basketmakers' Association and the Society of Designer Craftsmen, both of which have been supportive of my basketmaking ventures.

Many friends have helped me with this book, especially Mike Kidron and Mary Butcher, by reading and commenting on the text and generally egging me on. Last, but not least, Stefanie Foster, my editor at Quintet, and Ian Howes who took the photographs.

## BASKETMAKER CONTACTS AND SUPPLIERS

### UK
The Secretary of the
Basketmakers' Association
Ann Brooks
Pond Cottage
North Road
Chesham Bois
Bucks HP6 5NA

### USA
Mr Jim Widess
926 Gilman Street
Berkeley
California 94710

Mrs Judith Olney
34 Bradford Street
Rowley
MA 01969

Mrs Linda Lugenbill
361 Silver Springs Court
Colorado Springs
CO 80919

### CANADA
Ms Ankaret Dean
RRI McDonalds Corners
Ontario K0G 1MO

Mrs Joleen Gordon
121 Crichton Avenue
Dartmouth
Nova Scotia B3A 3R6

### AUSTRALIA
Mrs Sally King
PO Box 473
Ulverstone
Tasmania 7315

Mrs Jean Stone
Basketmakers of Victoria Inc
3 Loudon Road
Burwood
Victoria 3125

Thanks to Mrs Linda
Lugenbill for her help
and advice.

## FURTHER READING

Harvey, Virginia *The Techniques of Basketry* (Batsford)
Hoppe, Flo *Wicker Basketry* (Interweave Press)
La Plantz, Shereen *Plaited Basketry: The Woven Form* (Press de La Plantz)
Walpole, Lois *Creative Basketmaking* (Collins)
Wright, Dorothy *The Complete Book of Baskets and Basketry* (David & Charles)